重要表現を身につけて失礼のな

本書は、*Let's Learn Basic English for Co* ____ ey ／河合忠
仁）というロングセラー英語教材を改訂した ____ 、確実に学
習効果につながるという声を戴いた、シンプルながらもよく練られた構成と、例文の質の
良さ、実際によく使われる失礼のない表現の的確さにあったと考えています。改訂に際し
ては、そうした特長はそのままに、登場人物の変更、ダイアログ内の話題のアップデート、
練習問題の構成の一部変更をしました。

アメリカのカリフォルニア州から日本にやって来た留学生エマと同じ大学に通う大学生
のミサキのスーパーマーケットでの出会いから始まります。日本やアメリカの文化や社会、
習慣にまつわる事情の違いに直面しながら、彼女たちがお互いに疑問に思うことを質問し
合い、問題を提起する構成になっています。

日本では毎日大学や学校で英語を日常的に使用しているケースはほぼ稀ですが、英語は
日本から一歩外へ出れば、世界の共通語として使用されています。

しかし、日本の大学の中でも、さまざまな国から留学しに来ている友人が周囲にたくさ
んいるでしょう。重要な文法や表現を確実に自分のものにして応用するすべを身につけ、
英語でさまざまな国の人とやりとりをする中で、異文化を知り、より深く広い視野を身に
つけることは、これ以上ない生きる糧になります。

本書は 15 章構成で、

1 ダイアログ

2 ダイアログの一部の聞き取り

3 ダイアログで使用されている基本的かつ日常的表現法の確認

4 ダイアログで使用されている文法項目の復習と確認

5 ダイアログの内容や表現に関係する基本的な英作文

6 ダイアログの内容を少し発展させた英作文

という枠組みになっています。

Contents

Would you help me, please?

この章で学ぶこと 助けを求める表現
名詞の種類

次の会話を聴きましょう。 🔊 **Audio 02**

Emma: (At a supermarket) Excuse me. Do you speak English?

Misaki: Yes, but only a little.

Emma: Would you help me, please?

Misaki: O. K. What's your problem?

Emma: Here. I don't understand the meaning of this *kanji*. What is *kuro ushi* from Kagoshima?

Misaki: Oh, that's *kuro gyu*, not *kuro ushi*. It means "beef from black cows." Kagoshima is very famous for its black cows.

Emma: Oh, I see. Thank you.

 ▶ **meaning**：意味　▶ **cow**：雄牛　▶ **be famous for ~**：～で有名な

3

A Pick Up the Words

ダイアログを見ずに次の空欄を埋めなさい。

🔊 Audio 03

1. Excuse _____. Do you _____ English?

2. _____ you help me, _____?

3. O. K. _____ _____ problem?

4. I don't _____ the _____ of this *kanji*.

5. Kagoshima is very _____ for its black _____.

B Useful Expressions

助けを求める表現を学びましょう。ペアになって発音してみましょう。

🔊 Audio 04

1. **A:** Could you do me a favor?
   お願いがあるのですが。

   B: Sure. What can I do for you?
   いいですよ。なんでしょう。

2. **A:** Can I ask you a question?
   質問してもいいですか？

   B: Yes, certainly.
   はい、どうぞ。

3. **A:** Excuse me. Can you spare me a few minutes?
   すみません。少々お時間をいただいてもよろしいですか？

   B: OK. No problem.
   ええ。構いませんよ。

Check Grammar   名詞の種類の復習

日本語を参考にして、空欄に適語を入れなさい。

1. 私たちは 10 代の息子に困っている。

We have _____ with our teenage _____.

2. 私たちの国では、失業は深刻な問題です。

_____ is a serious _____ in our country.

3. それに意味はない。

_____ no _____ in that.

4. この漢字には 2 つの意味がある。

This Chinese _____ has two _____.

5. ローストビーフは、イギリスを代表する食べ物である。

Roast _____ is a typical English _____.

D   **Basic Composition**

日本語を英語にしましょう。音声を聴いて正解を確認しましょう。　　　🔊 **Audio 05**

1. （困っている人に対して）どうされましたか？

May I _____ _____?

2. （困っている人に対して）お困りのようですね。

You seem _____ _____ _____ _____.

3. この漢字の意味がわかりません。

I _____ no idea _____ _____ _____ _____ _____ _____.

4. 国産の肉は外国の肉よりも高い。

Japanese beef _____ _____ _____ _____ beef from abroad.

5. 奈良公園は鹿で有名です。

_____ _____ _____ _____ _____ _____ deer.

E Composition

（　）内の語を並べ替えて日本語に合う英語にしましょう。頭に来る単語の頭文字も小文字になっています。

1. 日本語を話す外国人の数は増加している。

The number _____.
(Japanese / foreigners / who / of / speak / increasing / is)

2. 日本にいるすべての外国人は英語を話す、とはかぎらない。

All _____ speak English.
(necessarily / Japan / do / foreigners / in / not)

3. ここがどこか教えてくれませんか？

_____ I am?
(you / tell / where / would / me)

4. アメリカの牛肉は日本への輸出が禁止された。

American beef _____ being _____.
(prohibited / was / from) (Japan / exported / to).

5. 私たちは国産の食材と外国の食材のどちらかを自由に選ぶことができる。

_____ domestic food ingredients
and foreign food ingredients.
(can / we / between / freely / choose)

No kidding. I can't believe it.

この章で学ぶこと 紹介の仕方の表現
現在完了形 (1)

次の会話を聴きましょう。　　　　　　　　　　　　🔊 Audio 06

Misaki: Hello, again. Have you finished shopping?

Emma: Yes. I've enjoyed shopping at this supermarket.

Misaki: I'm glad to hear it. My name is Misaki Tanaka. I'm a junior at Yamato University in Osaka.

Emma: Pardon? Did you say "Yamato University?" What a surprise! I'm an exchange student at that university.

Misaki: No kidding. I can't believe it.

Emma: My name is Emma Anderson. I'm from California. Call me Emma.

Misaki: Nice to meet you, Emma. I'm happy to meet you.

📋 **Notes** ▶ **junior**：四年制大学の 3 年生　▶ **Pardon**？：もう 1 度言ってください。
▶ **exchange student**：交換留学生　▶ **No kidding.**：冗談でしょ。

A Pick Up the Words

ダイアログを見ずに次の空欄を埋めなさい。

🔊 Audio 07

1. Hello, again. _____ you _____ shopping?

2. I'm a _____ at Yamato University in _____.

3. I'm an _____ _____ at that university.

4. _____ kidding. I can't _____ it.

5. I'm _____ to _____ you.

B Useful Expressions

紹介の仕方の表現を学びましょう。ペアになって発音してみましょう。

🔊 Audio 08

1. **A:** Let me introduce myself. My name is Misaki Tanaka.
   自己紹介させてください。私はタナカミサキと言います。

   B: My name is Emma Anderson.
   私はエマ・アンダーソンです。

2. **A:** Emma, this is my friend, Shota.
   エマ、私の友だちのショウタよ。

   B: Nice to meet you, Shota? I'm glad to meet you.
   初めまして、ショウタ。会えてうれしいわ。

3. **A:** Yuto, this is Ayaka Nishi.
   ユウト、こちらはニシアヤカさんよ。

   B: Hi! I've heard a lot about you from Reina.
   こんにちは！　あなたのことはレイナからいろいろ聞いています。

C Check Grammar 現在完了形（1）の復習

日本語を参考にして、空欄に適語を入れなさい。

1. 彼はちょうど今、車でここに来たところです。

He ＿＿＿＿＿＿＿ ＿＿＿＿＿＿＿ come here by car.

2. あなたは野口英世についてのお話をもう読みましたか？

Have you ＿＿＿＿＿＿＿ the story about Noguchi Hideyo
＿＿＿＿＿＿＿?

3. 私は人生においてこんなに美しい花を一度も見たことがない。

I have ＿＿＿＿＿＿＿ seen such a beautiful ＿＿＿＿＿＿＿ in my
life.

4. 彼女は今朝からずっと病気で寝ている。

She has ＿＿＿＿＿＿＿ sick in bed ＿＿＿＿＿＿＿ this morning.

5. あなたは全粒シリアルを食べたことがありますか？

Have you ＿＿＿＿＿＿＿ ＿＿＿＿＿＿＿ whole-grain cereal?

D Basic Composition

日本語を英語にしましょう。音声を聴いて正解を確認しましょう。　　🔊 Audio 09

1. 百貨店での買い物はどうでしたか？

＿＿＿＿＿ ＿＿＿＿＿ ＿＿＿＿＿ ＿＿＿＿＿ shopping at the department
store?

2. 私は大和大学の 4 年生です。

I'm ＿＿＿＿＿ ＿＿＿＿＿ ＿＿＿＿＿ Yamato University.

3. 私たちの大学には台湾からの留学生が何人かいる。

We ＿＿＿＿＿ ＿＿＿＿＿ ＿＿＿＿＿ ＿＿＿＿＿ from Taiwan in our
university.

4. 僕は斉木蓮です。斉木と呼んでください。

＿＿＿＿＿ ＿＿＿＿＿ ＿＿＿＿＿. ＿＿＿＿＿ ＿＿＿＿＿ ＿＿＿＿＿.

5. 私はアメリカ出身です。あなたはどこのご出身ですか？

_____ _____ _____. _____ _____ _____ _____?

E Composition

（　　）内の語を並べかえて日本語に合う英語にしましょう。大文字で始まる語句も小文字になっています。

1. 日本の多くのスーパーマーケットは夜遅くまで営業している。

Many supermarkets in Japan _____.
(the / late / are / until / evening / open / in)

2. 英語で自己紹介をする時、ファーストネームを先に言いますか？

When you _____, do you _____?
(yourself / in / introduce / English) (mention / name / your / first / first)

3. 海外からの多くの交換留学生にとって、日本語は最大の問題である。

Japanese _____
from abroad.
(problem / is / students / many / biggest / the / for / exchange)

4. "Pardon?" というのは「もう一度言ってくれませんか」という意味だ。

"Pardon?" means "_____,
please?"
(it / you / again / say / once / would)

5. 外国人と話をする時は彼らの目を見るべきだ。

When you _____, you _____.
(with / foreigners / talk) (their / at / look / eyes / should)

What are you studying at our university?

Unit

3

この章で学ぶこと 誘いの表現
受身形 (1)

次の会話を聴きましょう。 🔊 **Audio 10**

Misaki: I often drop in at this cafe. What would you like to drink?

Emma: Coffee is fine with me.

Misaki: (to the waitress) Two hot coffees, please. Emma, what are you studying in our university?

Emma: My major is Japanese literature. I'm especially interested in Lafcadio Hearn's life in Japan.

Misaki: Lafcadio Hearn? Don't ask me about him. What I know about him is that he lived in Japan, and got married to a Japanese woman. That's all.

Emma: You know him well enough. What is your major, Misaki?

Misaki: Chemistry. I'm interested in chemicals for foods and vegetables.

 Notes ▶ **drop in at ~**：〜に立ち寄る ▶ **hot coffee**：ホットコーヒー（和製英語）
▶ **major**：専門、専攻 ▶ **literature**：文学 ▶ **especially**：特に ▶ **Lafcadio Hearn**：文学者。ギリシャ生れのイギリス人で 1890 年来日、帰化。日本名は小泉八雲（1850–1904）。 ▶ **chemistry**：化学 ▶ **chemical**：化学薬品

11

A Pick Up the Words

ダイアログを見ずに次の空欄を埋めなさい。

Audio 11

1. I often _____ in at this _____.

2. What _____ you like to _____?

3. Emma, what are you _____ in our _____?

4. What I _____ about him is that he _____ in Japan.

5. I'm _____ in chemicals for _____ and vegetables.

B Useful Expressions

誘いの表現を学びましょう。ペアになって発音してみましょう。

Audio 12

1. **A:** Let's drop in at this cafe.
   このカフェにちょっと寄って行こうよ。

   B: OK. This cafe looks nice.
   いいね。このカフェよさそうだね。

2. **A:** Would you like to have some tea?
   お茶はいかがですか？

   B: Yes, please.
   はい、お願いします。

3. **A:** How about a Japanese dinner for a change?
   気分転換に和食の夕食はいかがですか？

   B: That's a good idea.
   いいですね。

Check Grammar 受身形（1）の復習

日本語を参考にして、（　　）に適語を入れなさい。

1. 彼女はそのニュースに驚いた。

She was _____ _____ the news.

2. あなたはあの新しい映画に興味がありますか？

_____ you _____ in that new movie?

3. 彼はすぐにその仕事に疲れるでしょう。

He will soon _____ tired _____ the work.

4. 私たちは母に 1 日家にいるように言われた。

We were _____ by our mother to stay at _____ all day long.

5. この本は夏目漱石によって書かれた。

This book _____ _____ by Natsume Soseki.

D **Basic Composition**

日本語を英語にしましょう。音声を聴いて正解を確認しましょう。　🔊 **Audio 13**

1. （お店で店員が）ご注文を承りましょうか？

May I _____ _____ _____?

2. コーヒーとベークド・チーズケーキを 1 つください。

I'll _____ _____ and _____ _____ _____ _____ _____.

3. どうして専門に心理学を選んだのですか？

_____ _____ _____ _____ _____ as your major?

4. ラフカディオ・ハーンは小泉節子と松江で結婚した。

Lafcadio Hearn _____ _____ _____ Koizumi Setsuko _____ _____.

Unit 3

5. あなたは農薬に関心があるのですか？

Are _____ _____ _____ _____ _____?

E Composition

（　　）内の語を並べかえて日本語に合う英語にしましょう。大文字で始まる語句も
小文字になっています。

1. 外国人の中には日本のコーヒー 1 杯の高い値段に驚いている人がいる。

Some foreigners are surprised _____
in Japan.
(the / high / of / at / of / cup / coffee / price / a)

2. 日本の多くの大学は研究よりも教育に重要性をおいている。

Many universities in Japan _____
than on research.
(on / importance / more / education / put)

3. ホラー小説がお好みならば、ハーンの『怪談』を読むべきです。

You _____ *Kwaidan* _____.
(should / Hearn's book / read) (you / horror / like / stories / if)

4. ハーンは大学で約 7 年間英文学を教えた。

Hearn _____
in universities.
(about / English / years / literature / taught / seven / for)

5. 野菜を育てるために、時には多くの農薬が使用される。

Sometimes _____ to grow
vegetables.
(used / lot / agricultural / a / chemicals / of / are)

Emma-san, welcome to our house.

この章で学ぶこと 相手をほめる表現
付加疑問文

次の会話を聴きましょう。　　　　　　　　　　　🔊 **Audio 14**

Misaki: Welcome to our house, Emma! See, our house is only a ten-minute walk from the supermarket. That means we live close together.

Emma: Yes, indeed. Misaki, your house looks lovely, and you have a beautiful Japanese-style garden.

Misaki: Thank you. My mother takes care of the trees. But don't ask me their names. Let's go inside the house.

Emma: Now, I have to take off my shoes here, don't I?

Misaki: That's right. Mom, this is Emma Anderson, an exchange student in our university. I told you I met her at the supermarket the other day. Emma, this is my mother, Yumiko.

Yumiko: Oh, yes. Emma-san. Welcome to our house. Please make yourself at home.

 Notes　▶ **take care of ~**：〜の世話をする　▶ **take off ~**：〜を脱ぐ
　　　　▶ **the other day**：先日　▶ **make oneself at home**：くつろぐ

A Pick Up the Words

ダイアログを見ずに次の空欄を埋めなさい。

Audio 15

1. Our _____ is only a ten-minute _____ from the supermarket.

2. You have a _____ Japanese-style _____.

3. My mother _____ care of the _____.

4. Now, I have to _____ off my _____ here, don't I?

5. Please _____ _____ at home.

B Useful Expressions

相手をほめる表現を学びましょう。ペアになって発音してみましょう。

Audio 16

1. **A:** You've got a lovely flower garden.
   すてきな花壇ですね。

   B: Thank you. Do you like flowers?
   ありがとう。花は好き？

2. **A:** You look nice in this sweater.
   君にはこのセーターが似合うね。

   B: Oh, thank you. I'm glad you like it.
   おー、どうもありがとう。それはうれしいよ。

3. **A:** Moe, you always make me happy.
   モエ、あなたはいつだって私を喜ばせてくれるわ。

   B: Oh, don't say that.
   えー、まさか。

Check Grammar 付加疑問文の復習

日本語を参考にして、空欄に適語を入れなさい。

1. あの男性はあなたのお兄さんですよね？

That man is _____ _____, _____ he?

2. あの少女たちは高校生ではありませんよね？

Those girls _____ high school students, are _____?

3. 田中さんは昨日私たちに会いに来ましたよね？

Mr. Tanaka came to _____ us yesterday, _____ he?

4. 私たちはそれほど上手に英語を話すことができませんよね？

We _____ speak English so _____, can we?

5. ここに座って映画を見ませんか？

Let's sit down here and _____ the movie, _____ we?

D **Basic Composition**

日本語を英語にしましょう。音声を聴いて正解を確認しましょう。 🔊 **Audio 17**

1. 私の会社は家から車で1時間です。

My office is _____ _____ _____ _____ _____ _____.

2. 電車で大阪に着くのに30分かかる。

It _____ _____ _____ _____ _____ _____ _____ _____
_____ train.

3. 父は庭の花の世話をするのが好きです。

_____ _____ _____ _____ _____ _____ _____
_____ in the garden.

4. 子供たちはコートを脱いで、テーブルの上に置いた。

The children _____ _____ _____ _____ and _____
_____ _____ _____ table.

5. 気楽にしてください。お茶はいかがですか？

_____ _____ _____ _____. _____ _____ _____

_____ _____ _____ tea?

E Composition

（　　）内の語を並べかえて日本語に合う英語にしましょう。大文字で始まる語句も小文字になっています。

1. このあたりでは多くの人が庭よりもガレージを欲しいと思っている。

Many people _____ around here.

(garages / want / rather / gardens / than)

2. あなたがフランス語で 2 単位取るのは難しい事かも知れない。

It may be a _____.

(for / for / credits / difficult / you / take / job / two / French / to)

3. これらの木を、樫の木や松の木のように、名前で覚えるようにしましょう。

_____, like an oak tree or a pine tree.

(to / by their name / let's / try / these / memorize / trees)

4. 部屋の中で帽子を脱ぐことは、かつて日本の道徳だった。

It used _____ in the room.

(be / to / a Japanese moral / cap / take / a / to / off)

5. 外国人を自宅に招待することはあなたにとって良い経験になるでしょう。

Inviting foreigners _____ you.

(your / to / will / for / be / good / a / house / experience)

How do you like our cafeteria?

この章で学ぶこと  驚きの表現
関係代名詞

次の会話を聴きましょう。 🔊 **Audio 18**

Emma: You've got nice school buildings and facilities on your campus.

Misaki: Oh, thank you for your compliment.

Emma: Your school library and cafeteria are the two places I visit every day. I'm happy I can use a computer all day long in the library.

Misaki: How do you like our cafeteria?

Emma: I was really surprised at the low prices of the foods they serve. And the taste is good. The coffee with *coffee fresh* they serve is also good.

Misaki: What do you think *coffee fresh* is made from?

Emma: Cream, I believe.

 Notes ▶ **facility**：施設 ▶ **compliment**：賛辞、お世辞 ▶ **serve ~**：（食べ物などを）出す

A Pick Up the Words

ダイアログを見ずに次の空欄を埋めなさい。

Audio 19

1. You've got nice school _____ and facilities on your _____.

2. Your school library and _____ are the two _____ I visit every day.

3. I'm _____ I can use a computer all day _____ in the library.

4. I was really _____ at the low prices of the foods they _____.

5. What do you _____ *coffee fresh* is made _____?

B Useful Expressions

驚きの表現を学びましょう。ペアになって発音してみましょう。

Audio 20

1. **A:** Long time no talk, isn't it?
   久々に話したよね？

   B: Yes, your e-mail yesterday really surprised me.
   うん、あなたの昨日のメールにはすごく驚いた。

2. **A:** Did you see the accident?
   その事故を目撃したんですか？

   B: Yes. That's why I was hardly surprised to hear the news.
   はい。だからそのニュースを聞いてもあまり驚かなかったんです。

3. **A:** He graduated from university with honors.
   彼は大学を優秀な成績で卒業しました。

   B: No wonder he knows everything.
   なるほど彼はすべてお見通しなわけです。

Check Grammar　関係代名詞の復習

日本語を参考にして、空欄に適語を入れなさい。

1. これは今朝私たちが訪れた体育館です。

This is the ＿＿＿＿＿＿＿ we ＿＿＿＿＿＿＿ this morning.

2. 先日私が買った電子辞書をあなたに見せましょう。

I'll show you the electronic ＿＿＿＿＿＿＿ I ＿＿＿＿＿＿＿ the other day.

3. この食堂で買える食べ物はおいしい。

The ＿＿＿＿＿＿＿ we can ＿＿＿＿＿＿＿ in this cafeteria are delicious.

4. 昨日あなたが私に話してくれた少年に、たった今会ったところです。

I've just met the ＿＿＿＿＿＿＿ you ＿＿＿＿＿＿＿ me about yesterday.

5. 現在の私は、あなたが私を初めて知った時の私ではない。

I'm not the man I ＿＿＿＿＿＿＿ when you knew me ＿＿＿＿＿＿＿.

D **Basic Composition**

日本語を英語にしましょう。音声を聴いて正解を確認しましょう。　🎧 **Audio 21**

1. あなたは私たちの大学をどう思いますか？

＿＿＿＿ ＿＿＿＿ ＿＿＿＿ ＿＿＿＿ ＿＿＿＿ ＿＿＿＿ university?

2. 私たちの図書館は朝 8 時から夜 10 時まで開館している。

Our library ＿＿＿＿ ＿＿＿＿ ＿＿＿＿ 8 ＿＿＿＿ ＿＿＿＿

＿＿＿＿ ＿＿＿＿ 10 in the evening.

3. 大学内ではどこでもあなたのコンピュータを使用していいですよ。

＿＿＿＿ ＿＿＿＿ ＿＿＿＿ ＿＿＿＿ ＿＿＿＿ ＿＿＿＿ anywhere

in the university.

4. 彼らが出してくれる食べ物の種類の豊富さに私は驚いた。

＿＿＿＿ ＿＿＿＿ ＿＿＿＿ ＿＿＿＿ the ＿＿＿＿ ＿＿＿＿

＿＿＿＿ they serve.

5. 彼らは国産の食材を使用しているのですか？

Are they ＿＿＿＿ ＿＿＿＿ ＿＿＿＿ ingredients?

E Composition

（　　）内の語を並べかえて日本語に合う英語にしましょう。大文字で始まる語句も
小文字になっています。

1. 大学への志願者をひきつけるために多くの新しい施設が建てられた。

A lot of new facilities ＿＿＿＿＿＿＿＿＿＿＿＿＿＿＿＿＿＿＿＿
university.
(for / built / attract / were / candidates / to)

2. もし学生が勉強に興味を持っていれば、彼らは図書館へしばしば行くかも知れない。

If the ＿＿＿＿＿＿＿＿＿＿＿＿＿＿＿＿, they ＿＿＿＿＿＿＿＿＿＿
often.
(in / are / interested / students / study) (the / may / library / visit)

3. 最近、多くの人々は食べ物の値段よりも食べ物の質を重要視する。
▶ set A above B を使用

Nowadays many people ＿＿＿＿＿＿＿＿＿＿＿＿＿＿＿＿＿＿＿
＿＿＿＿.
(the quality / of / above / food / food / set / the price of)

4. 「コーヒー・フレッシュ」は主に植物油と食品添加物で作られている。

Coffee fresh is made ＿＿＿＿＿＿＿＿＿＿＿＿＿＿＿＿＿＿＿＿.
(some / mainly / plant oil / from / and / food additives)

5. まず第一に、学校は生徒の健康に注意を払うべきだ。

First of all, ＿＿＿＿＿＿＿＿＿＿＿＿＿＿＿＿＿＿＿＿＿＿＿＿.
(should / schools / health / attention / students' / to / pay)

Many students have more interest in fashion.

この章で学ぶこと　同意する・同意しない表現
代名詞

次の会話を聴きましょう。　　　　　　　　　　　🔊 **Audio 22**

Misaki: What's your impression of the students on our campus, Emma?

Emma: All of the students look happy. They are well-dressed. And many coeds look as if they were out of the fashion magazines.

Misaki: Oh, do they? In fact, many students have more interest in fashion than in their study.

Emma: Tell me, Misaki. How do they earn money to buy their clothes? Do they work part-time?

Misaki: Some work as part-timers and others get money from their parents.

Emma: From their parents? Why are they so dependent on their parents? In America students try to become independent of their parents.

 Notes　▶ **impression**：印象　▶ **well-dressed**：身なりのきちんとした
▶ **coed**：女子学生　▶ **as if ~**：まるで〜かのように　▶ **earn ~**：〜を稼ぐ
▶ **dependent on ~**：〜に頼る　▶ **independent of ~**：〜に依存しない

23

A Pick Up the Words

ダイアログを見ずに次の空欄を埋めなさい。 Audio 23

1. What's your _____ _____ the students on our campus?

2. Many coeds _____ as if they were _____ of the fashion magazines.

3. Many students have more _____ in fashion _____ in their study.

4. How do they _____ money to buy their _____?

5. Some _____ as part-timers and others get money from their _____.

B Useful Expressions

同意する・同意しない表現を学びましょう。ペアになって発音してみましょう。 Audio 24

1. **A:** You seem to be happy today.
   今日はうれしそうだね。

   B: Oh, do I? I got 100 in the math exam.
   ああ、僕？　数学のテストで満点を取ったんだ。

2. **A:** Taiki hasn't arrived here yet.
   タイキはまだここに着いてないんだ。

   B: Be patient. Give him a few more minutes.
   我慢して。あともう数分待つことにしよう。

3. **A:** I think this T-shirt is expensive. Don't you think so?
   このTシャツは高いと思う。そう思わない？

   B: I agree with you.
   言う通りだね。

C Check Grammar 代名詞の復習

日本語を参考にして、空欄に適語を入れなさい。

1. 2 本の色鉛筆があります。1 本は赤で、もう 1 本は青です。

   There are two color pencils. _____ is red and the _____ is blue.

2. 双子の女の子だって。私はどちらがどちらか区別がつかない。

   The twin girls? I can't _____ one from the _____.

3. たくさんの花がある。白が数本あり、黄色も何本かある。

   There are a _____ of flowers. _____ are white, and others are yellow.

4. 私は電車で乗客を数人見た。1 人は女性で、他の乗客は男性だった。

   I saw several passengers on the train. _____ was a woman, and _____ others were men.

5. 知っていることと実行することはまったく別のことである。

   Knowing is one _____, and doing is quite _____.

D Basic Composition

日本語を英語にしましょう。音声を聴いて正解を確認しましょう。　　🔊 Audio 25

1. あなたの大阪の第一印象はどのようなものですか？

   What _____ _____ _____ _____ _____ Osaka?

2. 雨が降りそうな様子だ。

   It _____ _____ _____ it's _____ _____ rain.

3. ファッションと勉強は共に、多くの学生にとって重要である。

   Fashion and study are _____ _____ _____ _____ _____.

4. 学校の図書館でアルバイトをする学生もいる。

   Some students _____ _____ _____ _____ in the school library.

5. 多くの日本の学生は経済的に親に頼っている。

Many Japanese students _____ ___ _____ _____ _____.

E Composition

（　）内の語を並べかえて日本語に合う英語にしましょう。大文字で始まる語句も小文字になっています。

1. 最近、男性用化粧品がよく売れているそうですね。

I hear _____
recently.
(have / selling / cosmetics / men / been / well / for)

2. 若い女性が電車の中で化粧をしているのを私たちは時々見る。

We sometimes see some young women
_____.
(up / the / face / in / their / making / train)

3. アルバイトをすることによって、あなたは自分の新しい才能を発見するかもしれない。

_____
part-time.
(working / talent / may / your / you / new / by / find)

4. お金は大切であるが、それがすべてではない。

_____, _____.
(money / though / important / is) (is / everything / it / not)

5. 一部の日本の親は、できるだけ長く自分の子供と一緒に暮らしたいと思っている。

Some Japanese parents _____
possible.
(with / want / live / to / as / as / children / long / their)

Oh, that's a women-only car.

この章で学ぶこと 相づちの打ち方の表現
複文

次の会話を聴きましょう。　　　　　　　　　　　🔊 **Audio 26**

Emma: I think Japanese people are very patient in the crowded train during the rush hours.

Misaki: And they keep quiet even if they are pushed against other passengers.

Emma: Exactly. And very few say "Excuse me." Misaki, this morning during the rush hour I saw a strange car. There were only women in the car, and it wasn't so crowded. The other cars were crowded as usual.

Misaki: Oh, that's a women-only car. The idea is to protect women passengers from molesters.

Emma: I see. Wonderful Japanese culture, isn't it? But are there any molesters in crowded trains?

Misaki: I'm afraid there are. Be careful about molesters in the train.

📋 Notes ▶ **patient**：忍耐強い ▶ **crowded**：混雑した ▶ **even if ~**：たとえ～としても
▶ **passenger**：乗客 ▶ **protect ~**：～を守る ▶ **molester**：痴漢

27

A Pick Up the Words

ダイアログを見ずに次の空欄を埋めなさい。　　　　　　　　　🔊 Audio 27

1. I think Japanese _____ are very patient in the crowded

   _____.

2. They keep _____ even if they are _____ against other

   passengers.

3. This morning _____ the rush hour I saw a strange _____.

4. The _____ is to protect women passengers _____

   molesters.

5. Be _____ about molesters in the _____.

B Useful Expressions

相づちの打ち方の表現を学びましょう。ペアになって発音してみましょう。　🔊 Audio 28

1. **A:** Mt. Fuji is one of the most beautiful mountains in the world.
   富士山は世界でもっとも美しい山の一つなんだ。

   B: Do you really think so?
   本当にそう思ってるの？

2. **A:** We'll visit the museum tomorrow.
   僕たちは明日博物館に行くよ。

   B: Why not visit today? It may be closed tomorrow.
   今日行くのはどう？　明日は閉館しているかもしれない。

3. **A:** Finally our daughter will get married next week.
   ついに来週私たちの娘が結婚するんだよ。

   B: Yeah. I guess all of you will feel lonely.
   そう。あなたたちもさみしいだろうね。

C Check Grammar 複文の復習

日本語を参考にして、空欄に適語を入れなさい。

1. 彼は化学に非常な関心を持っていると私は思う。

   I _____ he has a great _____ in chemistry.

2. 私たちの学校はいつ設立されたか知っていますか？

   Do you _____ when our school was _____?

3. このワインは何から作られていると思いますか？

   _____ do you think this wine is made _____?

4. 彼はまるで小さな子供のようにふるまう。

   He behaves as _____ he were a little _____.

5. 私は彼が言ったことを理解できない。

   I can't _____ what he _____.

D Basic Composition

日本語を英語にしましょう。音声を聴いて正解を確認しましょう。　　🔊 Audio 29

1. 混雑した電車の中ではまったく動けない時がある。

   Sometimes you can't _____ _____ _____ _____
   _____ _____.

2. たとえ明日雨が降っても私は自転車で学校へ行く。

   I'll go to school _____ _____ _____ _____ _____
   _____ tomorrow.

3. 私たちのほとんどがその質問にすぐに答えることができなかった。

   Few of us _____ _____ _____ _____ _____.

4. 目的は子供たちにお金の節約の仕方を教えることです。

   The idea _____ to _____ _____ _____ _____ _____
   money.

5. 電車でスリにあわないように気をつけなさい。

Be careful _____ _____ _____ _____ _____ _____
on the train.

E Composition

（　　）内の語を並べかえて日本語に合う英語にしましょう。大文字で始まる語句も
小文字になっています。

1. 万一、電車の中で気分が悪くなったら、あなたはどうしますか？

_____, what would
you do?
(if / train / feel / you / sick / in / should / the)

2. 混んでいる電車の中でも本や新聞を読もうとする乗客がいる。

_____ even in the
crowded train.
(or / try / read / passengers / to / some / a book / newspaper)

3. 最近、多くの乗客は自分よりも年輩の人に席を譲らない。

Nowadays many passengers _____
_____.
(people / their / not / offer / older / seats / do / to / the)

4. 万一、他人の足を踏んだら、あなたは何と言いますか？

_____, what
would you say?
(on / if / another / you / step / of / the foot / person / should)

5. すべての乗客が楽に座れる電車が必要である。

We will need trains _____
_____.
(all / sit / passengers / the / where / can / easily)

Unit 8

Here, I can see no emergency phones.

この章で学ぶこと　確認の表現
受身形 (2)

次の会話を聴きましょう。　　　　　　🔊 **Audio 30**

Misaki: What do you think about our campus life, Emma?

Emma: Well, students seem to be enjoying their campus life very much. However, I was quite surprised to see so many students on the campus late in the evening. I simply can't believe this.

Misaki: What do you mean?

Emma: At my university in California, we were advised not to walk alone on the campus after dark, because it's dangerous.

Misaki: Is it true?

Emma: Yes, it is. And there are a lot of emergency phones installed on the campus. But here, I can see no emergency phones. What a safe country!

 Notes ▶ **simply**：まったく　▶ **were advised**：忠告された
▶ **emergency phone**：非常救急電話　▶ **installed**：設置されている

A Pick Up the Words

ダイアログを見ずに次の空欄を埋めなさい。

Audio 31

1. What do you _____ _____ our campus life?

2. Students _____ to be _____ their campus life very much.

3. I was _____ surprised to see so many students on the campus _____ in the evening.

4. We were advised not to _____ alone on the campus after _____.

5. There are a _____ of emergency phones installed _____ the campus.

B Useful Expressions

確認の表現を学びましょう。ペアになって発音してみましょう。

Audio 32

1. **A:** What do you mean, our bus isn't moving?
   私たちの (乗る) バスは動いていないということですか？

   B: I'm sorry it's broken down.
   申し訳ありませんが、故障しています。

2. **A:** Make sure that all the windows are closed.
   すべての窓が閉まっているか必ず確認してください。

   B: OK. I will.
   はい。そうします。

3. **A:** Are you sure you really want to join the company?
   本当にその会社に就職したいんですか？

   B: Yes, absolutely.
   はい、そうなんです。

C Check Grammar 受身形（2）の復習

日本語を参考にして、空欄に適語を入れなさい。

1. 私たちの学校では日本語が 10 年間教えられている。

Japanese has _____ taught _____ ten years in our school.

2. あなたは試験の結果に満足していますか？

Are you _____ _____ the result of the exam?

3. 私たちの秘密は皆に知られている。

Our secret is _____ _____ everybody.

4. 彼は良い弁護士だと言われている。

He is _____ to _____ a good lawyer.

5. 喜んでいつでもあなたのお手伝いをします。

I'll be _____ to _____ you anytime.

D Basic Composition

日本語を英語にしましょう。音声を聴いて正解を確認しましょう。　　🔊 **Audio 33**

1. 私たちの大学についてのあなたの意見はどうですか？

_____ _____ _____ _____ _____ our university?

2. 父の声が遠くからやってくるように思えた。

Father's voice seemed to be _____ _____ _____ _____.

3. 数人の学生が道路に座っているのを見て、私は驚いた。

I was surprised to see _____ _____ _____ _____
_____ _____.

4. 外国では、生水を飲まないように私は忠告された。

I was _____ _____ _____ _____ unboiled _____ in a
foreign country.

5. 日本は本当に安全な国であるというのは真実ですか？

_____ _____ _____ that _____ _____ really _____

_____ _____?

E Composition

（　　）内の語を並べかえて日本語に合う英語にしましょう。大文字で始まる語句も小文字になっています。

1. 学校は学生が楽しめる場所でなければならない。

School must be _____.
(students / the place / themselves / enjoy / where / can)

2. 快適な環境を増大させるため、多くの大学にはきれいで美しいトイレがある。

Many universities _____ the amenities.
(and / to / clean / beautiful / increase / have / toilets)

3. 学生は自分たちが持っている自由な時間を最大限利用するようにすべきである。

Students _____
they have.
(best / try / the / to / of / make / should / use / free time)

4. アメリカの大学では、キャンパスの巡回は犯罪を防ぐための重要な手段である。

In American universities, campus patrols _____

_____.
(crime / important / an / to / are / prevent / means)

5. 統計によると、アメリカにおけるキャンパスでの犯罪率は非常に高い。

According to the statistics, _____

_____ .
(is / in America / extremely / on-campus / rate / high / crime)

Students won't be able to learn English.

この章で学ぶこと 会話を始める表現
to 不定詞

次の会話を聴きましょう。　　　　　　　　　　　　　🔊 **Audio 34**

Misaki: What's new, Emma? You look a little excited.

Emma: I am. You know, this morning, I was invited by Prof. Yamada, my English teacher, to observe his general English class. It was very interesting to me.

Misaki: Tell me about it.

Emma: There were more than 40 students in his class. So many students in a language class. And there was no student-to-student communication in English. Some students in the back of the classroom were sleeping.

Misaki: Was Prof. Yamada using English in class?

Emma: Yes, he was. But what is important is that students must learn English, not the teacher. Students won't be able to learn English if they don't try to use it as often as possible.

📋 **Notes** ▶ **observe ~**：〜を参観する ▶ **general English class**：一般教養英語
▶ **as often as possible**：できるだけ頻繁に

A Pick Up the Words

ダイアログを見ずに次の空欄を埋めなさい。 🔊 Audio 35

1. What's _____, Emma? You look a little _____.

2. I was _____ by Prof. Yamada to _____ his general English class.

3. _____ me _____ it.

4. There were _____ _____ 40 students in his class.

5. What is _____ is that students must learn English, not the _____.

B Useful Expressions

会話を始める表現を学びましょう。ペアになって発音してみましょう。 🔊 Audio 36

1. **A:** Hi, Emily. What's new?
   やあ、エミリー。最近どう？

   B: Nothing special.
   特に何もないわ。

2. **A:** You know, Yuka had a baby last month.
   ねえ、ユウカが先月出産したの。

   B: Oh, she must be very happy.
   わあ、彼女はとても幸せでしょうね。

3. **A:** Say, Shota, what's the airmail postage to Germany?
   なあ、ショウタ、ドイツへの航空郵便料金っていくら？

   B: Sorry, I have no idea.
   ごめん、わからない。

C Check Grammar   to 不定詞の復習

日本語を参考にして、空欄に適語を入れなさい。

1. 私は昨日友だちに誕生日プレゼントを買うのを忘れた。

I _____ to buy a birthday _____ for my friend yesterday.

2. うそを言うことはいつでも悪いことですか？

Is it always _____ to tell a _____?

3. 私たちは外国の人々とコミュニケーションをとるために英語を学ぶ。

We _____ English to communicate _____ people in foreign countries.

4. 私たちは食べるために生きるのですか、それとも生きるために食べるのですか？

_____ we live to eat _____ eat to live?

5. リクは大人になって高校の教員になった。

Riku _____ up to _____ a high school teacher.

D Basic Composition

日本語を英語にしましょう。音声を聴いて正解を確認しましょう。   🔊 Audio 37

1. 「調子はどう？」「元気にやってるよ。」

"_____ _____ _____ _____ with you?" "_____ _____."

2. 今からあなたのしたいことを私に言ってください。

_____ _____ _____ _____ would like to do _____ _____.

3. 彼らは幸運にも、その変化がどのように起こったのかを観察することができた。

They were lucky _____ _____ _____ the _____ _____ _____.

4. 一部の学生は授業中メールを送ることに忙しい。

_____ _____ are busy sending _____ _____ _____.

5. 驚くべきなのは、一部の保育園で英語が教えられ始めたことである。

What is surprising _____ that _____ _____ _____
_____ _____ at some nursery schools.

E Composition

（　　）内の語を並べかえて日本語に合う英語にしましょう。大文字で始まる語句も小文字になっています。

1. 時には、大学の授業は一般に公開すべきである。

Sometimes university classes _____.
(open / the / be / to / should / public)

2. 外国語を学べば、さまざまな方法で世界を見ることができるかもしれない。

If we learn a foreign language, _____
_____.
(to / in a / may / able / look / be / different / at / we / the world /
way)

3. 英語の授業は、英語を学びたい人に対して行われるほうが良いかもしれない。

It may be better to give _____
English.
(want / English / to / learn / those / classes / who / to)

4. 大学では英語教育のはっきりした目的を持つことが必要である。

It is necessary _____
in university.
(purpose / a / to / teaching English / clear / have / of)

5. 高校の復習をあまりに強調しすぎると、学生は大学生活に興味を失うかもしれない。

If you emphasize _____, _____
university life.
(much / high school / too / reviews) (may / in / students / interest /
lose)

Tell me about Hearn in one word.

この章で学ぶこと

希望や願いの表現
接続詞

次の会話を聴きましょう。　　　　　　　　　　　　　🔊 Audio 38

Misaki: Emma, what do you think about your seminar teacher?

Emma: Misaki, I'm so happy I could come to this university. She knows a lot about Hearn. Sometimes she gives a lecture on Hearn in her class.

Misaki: Do you understand her Japanese?

Emma: I hope so. I can guess what she is talking about because I have some basic knowledge about Lafcadio Hearn.

Misaki: You are a genius! Emma, tell me about Hearn in one word.

Emma: That's difficult, but I think he tried to show Japanese soul in his writings. Have you ever read his "Ghost Story?" It is fantastic!

 Notes　▶ **lecture**：講義　▶ **basic knowledge**：基礎知識　▶ **genius**：天才
　　　　　▶ **soul**：魂　▶ **fantastic**：すばらしい

A Pick Up the Words

ダイアログを見ずに次の空欄を埋めなさい。

Audio 39

1. I'm so _____ I could come to this _____.

2. Sometimes she _____ a _____ on Hearn in her class.

3. I can guess _____ she is talking _____.

4. Emma, _____ me about Hearn in one _____.

5. I think he tried to _____ Japanese _____ in his writings.

B Useful Expressions

希望や願いの表現を学びましょう。ペアになって発音してみましょう。

Audio 40

1. **A:** We are expecting to talk with the president tomorrow.
   私たちは明日社長と話せると思います。

   B: How nice!
   すばらしい！

2. **A:** I'll have a French test next period. Cross your fingers for me.
   次の時限でフランス語のテストがあるんだ。私の幸運を祈って。

   B: By all means.
   もちろん。

3. **A:** I hope to see you again soon.
   またすぐにお会いしたいです。

   B: So do I.
   私もです。

Check Grammar 接続詞の復習

日本語を参考にして、空欄に適語を入れなさい。

1. 彼は野菜が好きではないので、野菜を食べない。

He doesn't eat vegetables _____ he doesn't like _____.

2. 私は疲れていたのでいつもより早く寝た。

I was tired, _____ I went to bed _____.

3. あなたは家にいても良いし、私たちと一緒に来ても良いですよ。

You may stay at home _____ you may _____ with us.

4. パーティで彼女と話すことができてうれしかった。

I was _____ I could _____ with her at the party.

5. 困ったことに、私たちには時間が足りなくなってきています。

The _____ is we are getting _____ of time.

D **Basic Composition**

日本語を英語にしましょう。音声を聴いて正解を確認しましょう。 📶 Audio 41

1. 私はこの大学の学生であることがうれしい。

I'm _____ _____ _____ _____ _____ in this university.

2. 彼女は宗教について学生に講義をした。

She _____ _____ _____ _____ _____ _____ _____ _____ religion.

3. 食卓で私たちはお互いに一言も発しなかった。

At the table _____ _____ _____ _____ _____ _____ _____.

4. 芸術についてほとんど知識がないということを言うのは恥ずかしい。

I'm ashamed to _____ _____ _____ _____ _____ _____ _____.

5. シェイクスピアの作品のどれかを今までに読んだことがありますか？

Have you _____ _____ _____ _____ _____ _____?

E Composition

（　　）内の語を並べかえて日本語に合う英語にしましょう。大文字で始まる語句も小文字になっています。

1. 文学は、言語で内面の世界を表わす芸術作品かもしれない。

Literature may be _____

language.

(world / in / works of art / the / show / inner / to)

2. 私は若者が使う日本語を理解できない。

I can't _____.

(people / understand / young / the Japanese / use / which)

3. 大学教育の１つの目的は人生についての基礎知識を増やすことである。

One purpose of university education _____

_____.

(about / to / basic / is / knowledge / life / increase)

4. 外国人が日本人の考え方を理解できないと考えるのは間違っている。

It is wrong to think that _____

_____.

(of / understand / foreigners / way / the Japanese / thinking / can't)

5. 日本人より日本をよく知っている外国人がいる。

There are some foreigners _____

_____.

(Japanese / know / Japan / better / who / than / people)

11 Don't ask me about it, either.

この章で学ぶこと　**心配して尋ねる表現**
命令文

What's the matter?

次の会話を聴きましょう。　🔊 **Audio 42**

Misaki: Hi, Emma! You don't look happy today. What's the matter with you?

Emma: I'm OK. I was just wondering why many Japanese students are not interested in politics.

Misaki: Come on, Emma! Don't be so serious. Explain yourself if you like.

Emma: About an hour ago I asked some of my literature classmates about "Young people voting in Japan."

Misaki: Oh, how did they respond to you?

Emma: They told me they didn't know much about the problem.

Misaki: Don't ask me about it, either. I'm a nonpolitical student, you know.

 Notes　▶ **politics**：政治　▶ **explain oneself**：自分の考えをはっきりと説明する
▶ **respond to ~**：〜に反応する　▶ **nonpolitical**：政治に無関心の、ノンポリの

A Pick Up the Words

ダイアログを見ずに次の空欄を埋めなさい。 Audio 43

1. What's the _____ _____ you?

2. _____ on, Emma! Don't be so _____.

3. Explain _____ if you _____.

4. They told me they _____ know much about the _____.

5. _____ ask me _____ it, either.

B Useful Expressions

心配して尋ねる表現を学びましょう。ペアになって発音してみましょう。 Audio 44

1. **A:** You look pale. What's wrong with you?
   顔色が悪いよ。どうしたの？

   B: I have a temperature and I feel cold.
   熱があって寒気がするんだ。

2. **A:** What's your trouble?
   いったいどうしたの？

   B: Homework. I can't finish it by tomorrow.
   宿題。明日までに終わらせられない。

3. **A:** What's eating you, Shota? Calm down.
   何をいらいらしてるの、ショウタ？　落ち着いて。

   B: His report. It isn't true.
   彼のレポート。それはにせものだ。

C Check Grammar 命令文の復習

日本語を参考にして、空欄に適語を入れなさい。

1. また私たちの会議に遅れないでください。

Don't _____ late for our _____ again.

2. ここに来て、座ってください。

Do _____ here, and _____ down.

3. あなたの電子辞書を私に見せてください。

_____ me have a _____ at your electronic dictionary.

4. このコンピュータに絶対触ってはいけないよ！

Don't _____ dare _____ this computer!

5. 急いでください、そうしないと最終電車に乗り遅れますよ。

_____ up, or you'll _____ the last train.

D Basic Composition

日本語を英語にしましょう。音声を聴いて正解を確認しましょう。　🔊 **Audio 45**

1. 今日は元気がないようですね。どうかされたのですか？

You _____ _____ today. Is _____ _____ _____ _____?

2. なぜ彼女はあんな質問をしたのでしょう。

I _____ _____ _____ _____ such a question.

3. 手短に自分の考えを説明してくれませんか？

_____ _____ _____ _____ briefly?

4. さあ！　失望しないで。もう1回やってみなさい。

_____ _____! _____ _____ _____. Try it once again.

5. 残念ながら、その問題について私は何も知りません。

_____ _____ I _____ _____ _____ _____ the problem.

E Composition

（　　）内の語を並べかえて日本語に合う英語にしましょう。大文字で始まる語句も小文字になっています。

1. ほとんどの学生は政治や社会の問題に関心を持っていないように思える。

Few students _____ have _____ or social problems.
(in / to / interest / seem / political)

2. 国家とは何かということを、あなたは今まで考えたことがありますか？

_____ a nation is?
(you / what / ever / thought / have)

3. 世界の人々が日本人と同じ価値観を持っていると考えてはいけない。

Don't think that people in the world _____ _____ Japanese people do.
(the / as / same / have / value)

4. 言語によって他の人々ときちんとコミュニケーションをとる方法を私たちは学ばなければならない。

We have to learn _____ properly _____ by language.
(to / people / communicate / how / other / with)

5. オンライン・ニュース・マガジンを毎日読むようにしましょうか。

_____ everyday?
(we / read / news / shall / try / magazine / to / online)

But farmers need this rain badly.

この章で学ぶこと  推量・推測の表現
感嘆文

次の会話を聴きましょう。　　　　　　　　　　🔊 **Audio 46**

Emma: What nasty rain! It's been raining for a week.

Misaki: This rainy season will last two more weeks, I guess. Floods may occur somewhere in Japan.

Emma: Oh, no. I don't like rain. Moreover, I can't put up with this humidity.

Misaki: But farmers need this rain badly in order to grow rice plants. Have you noticed the paddy fields near your apartment?

Emma: Yes. I saw one or two small farming trucks moving in the fields in the rain. What were they doing?

Misaki: They were planting rice in the rain.

📋 Notes ▶ **nasty**：いやな　▶ **rainy season**：梅雨　▶ **flood**：洪水
▶ **put up with ~**：〜に我慢する　▶ **humidity**：湿気
▶ **badly**：非常に、どうしても　▶ **in order to ~**：〜のために
▶ **rice plant**：稲　▶ **notice ~**：〜に気づく　▶ **paddy field**：田んぼ
▶ **plant ~**：〜を植える

A Pick Up the Words

ダイアログを見ずに次の空欄を埋めなさい。

🔊 Audio 47

1. What _____ rain! It's _____ raining for a week.

2. This rainy _____ will _____ two more weeks, I guess.

3. I can't _____ _____ _____ this humidity.

4. _____ need this rain badly in order to _____ rice plants.

5. _____ you noticed the paddy fields _____ your apartment?

B Useful Expressions

推量・推測の表現を学びましょう。ペアになって発音してみましょう。

🔊 Audio 48

1. **A:** I guess Mr. Yamada will be busy this afternoon.
   山田さんは今日の午後は忙しいことと思います。

   B: Yes, he is supposed to attend the meeting at two o'clock.
   はい、彼は 2 時に会議に出席することになっています。

2. **A:** Don't worry. He will soon change his mind.
   心配しないで。彼はすぐに気が変わるよ。

   B: I suppose you are right.
   あなたの言う通りだと思う。

3. **A:** I imagine the traffic is very heavy now.
   今は交通渋滞が激しいと思うなあ。

   B: Then, I'll stay here another hour.
   じゃあ、もう 1 時間ここにいよう。

C Check Grammar 感嘆文の復習

日本語を参考にして、空欄に適語を入れなさい。

1. これはなんて熱いコーヒーなんでしょう！

_____ hot coffee _____ is!

2. 洪水はなんて恐ろしいんだろう！

_____ terrible the flood _____!

3. あなたはなんて良い考えを思いつくのでしょう！

_____ a good _____ you have!

4. ああ、私はどれだけ甘いものに目がないんだ！

Oh, _____ I _____ sweets!

5. なんてスピードであなたは運転しているんだ！　私は怖い。

How _____ you are _____! I'm scared.

D Basic Composition

日本語を英語にしましょう。音声を聴いて正解を確認しましょう。　🔊 Audio 49

1. ついに梅雨が始まった。

Finally the _____ _____ _____ set in.

2. 災害はまったく予期していない時に起こる。

Disaster _____ _____ it is least expected.

3. 私は彼らの言動に我慢できない。

I can't _____ _____ _____ their behavior.

4. クラブ活動を楽しむために学校へ行く生徒もいる。

Some students go to school _____ _____ _____ enjoy
their club activities.

5. 私たちは彼がグラウンドでテニスをしているのを見た。

We _____ _____ _____ tennis on the ground.

E Composition

（　）内の語を並べかえて日本語に合う英語にしましょう。大文字で始まる語句も小文字になっています。

1. 「スロー・フード運動」は 1986 年イタリアの小さな村で始められた。

"Slow Food Campaign" _____ in 1986.
(a / at / was / Italy / small / in / started / village)

2. この運動の目的は地元の食材と食文化を守ることである。

The idea _____ ingredients and local food culture.
(of / local / food / campaign / is / to / this / protect)

3. 異常気象が原因で、雨が降ると、しばしば土砂降りになる。

Because of unusual weather, _____.
(when / often / it / it / pours / rains)

4. そのレポートによれば、日本の米の自給率は 95％である。

According to the report, _____ 95%.
(is / self-sufficiency / for / rate / Japan's / rice)

5. 約 3 千年前に、米は中国から日本にもたらされたと言われている。

It is said _____ about 3,000 years ago.
(Japan / rice / brought / China / to / that / was / from)

How can they keep studying all day long?

この章で学ぶこと  会話のつなぎの表現 (1)
感覚動詞

次の会話を聴きましょう。　　　　　　　　　　　　　　　🔊 **Audio 50**

Emma: May I ask you a question?

Misaki: Sure, go ahead. What is it?

Emma: When I come home from school around ten in the evening, I very often see on the station platform some elementary school children talking cheerfully or eating something. What are they doing there?

Misaki: Emma, they are on their way home from *juku*, a private cram school where they study after school is over.

Emma: After school is over? Incredible! How can they keep studying all day long? Don't they have time to enjoy themselves?

Misaki: Well, that's a difficult question. I can't say "Yes" or "No" in a simple word.

 ▶ **go ahead**：どうぞ　▶ **elementary school**：小学校
▶ **cheerfully**：楽しそうに　▶ **incredible**：信じられない

A Pick Up the Words

ダイアログを見ずに次の空欄を埋めなさい。 Audio 51

1. I very often see on the _____ platform some elementary school

   _____ talking cheerfully.

2. They are on _____ way _____ from *juku*.

3. _____ can they keep _____ all day long?

4. Don't they _____ time to _____ themselves?

5. I _____ say "Yes" or "No" in a simple _____.

B Useful Expressions

会話のつなぎの表現（1）を学びましょう。ペアになって発音してみましょう。 Audio 52

1. **A:** I went to the department store yesterday.
   昨日デパートに行ったんだ。

   B: Oh, did you? What did you buy?
   へえ、そうだったの？　何を買ったの？

2. **A:** I like *Ieyasu* very much.
   僕は家康がとても好きなんだ。

   B: That reminds me. I have to read a book about him.
   それで思い出した。彼についての本を読まなきゃいけない。

3. **A:** Do you mind if I use your car this afternoon?
   今日の午後あなたの車を使っても構いませんか？

   B: Of course not. Go right ahead.
   もちろん。どうぞ。

52 How can they keep studying all day long?

Check Grammar　感覚動詞の復習

日本語を参考にして、空欄に適語を入れなさい。

1. 私はかわいらしい鳥が庭でさえずっているのを見た。

I ＿＿＿＿＿＿ a pretty bird ＿＿＿＿＿＿ in the garden.

2. 私たちは昨夜家が少し揺れるのを感じた。

We felt our ＿＿＿＿＿＿ shake a ＿＿＿＿＿＿ last night.

3. 彼が部屋から出て行くのが聞こえましたか？

Did you ＿＿＿＿＿＿ him ＿＿＿＿＿＿ out of his room?

4. 私は彼が通りを横切るのを見かけた。

I saw ＿＿＿＿＿＿ walk across the ＿＿＿＿＿＿.

5. あなたはちょっと前に自分の名前が呼ばれるのが聞こえませんでしたか？

Didn't you ＿＿＿＿＿＿ your name called a moment ＿＿＿＿＿＿?

D Basic Composition

日本語を英語にしましょう。音声を聴いて正解を確認しましょう。　📶 **Audio 53**

1. 私は私たちの猫が庭の塀の上を歩くのを見た。

I ＿＿＿＿＿ ＿＿＿＿＿ ＿＿＿＿＿ ＿＿＿＿＿ on the wall of the garden.

2. あなたはいつも何時に学校から帰ってきますか？

What time do you usually ＿＿＿＿＿ ＿＿＿＿＿ ＿＿＿＿＿ ＿＿＿＿＿?

3. 私たちは市役所に行く途中です。

We're ＿＿＿＿＿ ＿＿＿＿＿ ＿＿＿＿＿ ＿＿＿＿＿ the city office.

4. これが 20 年前に私が生まれた病院です。

＿＿＿＿＿ ＿＿＿＿＿ ＿＿＿＿＿ ＿＿＿＿＿ ＿＿＿＿＿ I was born 20 years ago.

5. 混雑したバスの中で、どうやったら立ち続けられますか？

_____ _____ _____ _____ _____ in the crowded bus?

E Composition

（　　）内の語を並べかえて日本語に合う英語にしましょう。大文字で始まる語句も小文字になっています。

1. 多くの小学生は有名中学校の入試にのぞむために塾に通う。

Many pupils _____ to famous junior high schools.
(entrance / try / exams / to/ attend / *juku*)

2. たいていは小学生が 4 年生になる時に塾に通い始める。

Usually pupils start attending *juku* _____
_____.
(they / year / their / when / reach / fourth)

3. 親が金持ちでなければ、その子供たちは塾に通えないだろう。

_____, their children would not attend *juku*.
(parents / rich / if / enough / are / the / not)

4. 塾は小学生が勉強の仕方を学ぶところである、と一部の人は言う。

Some people say *juku* is a place _____
_____.
(study / will / learn / where / pupils / to / how)

5. 何時かしら。

_____.

I (it / time / wonder / what / is)

14

I feel more at home reading in English.

この章で学ぶこと 会話のつなぎの表現 (2)
動名詞

次の会話を聴きましょう。 🔊 **Audio 54**

Emma: Misaki, you always speak good English. Tell me how you learned English.

Misaki: To tell you the truth, my father taught me English intensively at home for five years when I was in my early teens. But now I have forgotten most of my English.

Emma: Oh, it's a shame. Don't you read books on chemistry in English?

Misaki: Sometimes I have to, but reading in English is different from speaking in English. I feel more at home when I'm reading in English. Emma, your Japanese is much better than my English.

Emma: Thank you. By the way I've found some native English teachers in Yamato University don't learn Japanese. I wonder why.

Misaki: Well, the answer is simple. English is the common world language, and Japanese is still a minor language, you know.

📋 Notes ▶ **To tell you the truth**：実は ▶ **intensively**：集中的に
▶ **early teens**：10 代の初め ▶ **it's a shame**：それは残念です
▶ **feel at home**：気が楽である ▶ **minor**：(量などが) 少ない、少数派の

A Pick Up the Words

ダイアログを見ずに次の空欄を埋めなさい。　🔊 Audio 55

1. My _____ taught me English intensively at _____.

2. _____ you read _____ on chemistry in English?

3. _____ in English is _____ from speaking in English.

4. I've _____ some native English teachers don't _____ Japanese.

5. Japanese is _____ a minor language, you _____.

B Useful Expressions

会話のつなぎの表現（2）を学びましょう。ペアになって発音してみましょう。🔊 Audio 56

1. **A:** Oh, by the way, Nanami called you while you were out.
   ねえ、ところで、あなたの不在中にナナミが電話してきたよ。

   B: Thank you. I'll call her back in a minute.
   ありがとう。すぐに彼女に折り返すよ。

2. **A:** How did he write this essay?
   彼はこのエッセイをどうやって書いたの？

   B: To tell you the truth, I'm not sure.
   実は、僕にはわからないんだ。

3. **A:** You can drive a car, can't you?
   あなたは車を運転できたよね？

   B: No. As a matter of fact, I don't have a driver's license.
   いえ。実を言うと運転免許を持っていないんです。

Check Grammar　動名詞の復習

日本語を参考にして、空欄に適語を入れなさい。

1. 百聞は一見にしかず、というのは本当ですか？

Is it _____ that seeing is _____?

2. 母はパーティの準備でずっと忙しい。

My mother has been _____ _____ for the party.

3. 私たちはみんなスキーとスケートが好きです。

We are all _____ of skiing and _____.

4. あの映画は見る価値があると私は思う。

I think that _____ is worth _____.

5. 私は彼にひと月前に会ったことを覚えていた。

I _____ seeing him a _____ ago.

D Basic Composition

日本語を英語にしましょう。音声を聴いて正解を確認しましょう。　🔊 **Audio 57**

1. 実は、私はオムレツが好きではない。

_____ _____ _____ _____, I don't like omelettes.

2. 私は 10 代の初めの頃、フランスで両親と暮らしていた。

I lived with my parents in France _____ _____ _____ _____.

3. あなたがそんなに早く出発しなければいけないなんて残念です。

It's a _____ _____ _____ _____ _____ so soon.

4. スーツを着るよりもブルージーンズをはいているほうが気が楽です。

I _____ _____ _____ _____ in blue jeans than in a suit.

5. 関西の日本語は、関東の日本語と異なる。

Japanese in the Kansai area _____ _____ _____
_____ _____ the Kanto area.

E Composition

（　　）内の語を並べかえて日本語に合う英語にしましょう。大文字で始まる語句も
小文字になっています。

1. 外国語を学ぶ時は、それを集中的に学んだほうが良い。

When you learn a foreign language, _____
_____.

(learn / intensively / better / it / had / you)

2. 私たちが非常に幼い頃学んだものは、めったに忘れない。

_____ when we were very
young.

(seldom / forget /we / we / learned / what)

3. 英語は日本の小学校で教科として教えられている。

English is _____.
(as / Japan / a subject / elementary / taught / school / in / in)

4. 世界で約 365 万の人々が日本語を学んでいる。

About 3,650,000 _____.
(are / in / learning / the / people / world / Japanese)

5. 日本語を学ぶ 1 つの目的は、将来良い仕事に就くことです。

_____ in the
future.
(a / is / learning / job / of / good / one / purpose / Japanese / to /
get)

15 I'll never forget your kindness.

この章で学ぶこと  感謝の表現
現在完了形 (2)

次の会話を聴きましょう。　　　　　　　　　　　　　🔊 **Audio 58**

Misaki: Emma, you look so excited. What's happened to you?

Emma: Misaki, I'm so happy. Yesterday I received a letter from Sokei University in Tokyo. It said they would give me a scholarship to study on their graduate course from April. My thesis "The Life of Lafcadio Hearn in Matsue" was accepted.

Misaki: Congratulations! Are there any famous Hearn scholars in that university?

Emma: Yes. There are two professors who are world-famous.

Misaki: Then, in two months we have to say good-bye to each other. I hope we can get together again after April if we have time.

Emma: Definitely. I'll never forget the kindness you have shown to me for the past ten months.

 Notes ▶ **scholarship**：奨学金　▶ **graduate course**：大学院
▶ **was accepted**：受理された　▶ **congratulations**：おめでとう
▶ **get together**：集まる　▶ **definitely**：もちろん

A Pick Up the Words

ダイアログを見ずに次の空欄を埋めなさい。　　　　　　　　　　　🔊 Audio 59

1. _____ I received a _____ from Sokei University in Tokyo.

2. Are _____ any _____ Hearn scholars in that university?

3. In two _____ we have to say good-bye to _____ other.

4. I hope we can get _____ again after April _____ we have time.

5. I'll _____ forget the kindness you have _____ to me.

B Useful Expressions

感謝の表現を学びましょう。ペアになって発音してみましょう。　　🔊 Audio 60

1. **A:** Thank you for inviting me for dinner.
   ディナーに招待してくれてありがとう。

   B: It's our pleasure.
   どういたしまして。

2. **A:** I'm very grateful to you for your kindness.
   あなたのご親切にとても感謝しています。

   B: Don't mention it.
   どういたしまして。

3. **A:** I appreciate everything you have done for me.
   あなたがしてくれたすべてに感謝しています。

   B: You're welcome.
   どういたしまして。

C Check Grammar 現在完了形（2）の復習

日本語を参考にして、空欄に適語を入れなさい。

1. 私は人生で 1 度も太平洋上を飛んだことがない。

I have _____ flown over the Pacific Ocean in my _____.

2. 私たちはこの町に 3 年間住んでいる。

We have _____ in this town _____ three years.

3. 何をずっと書いているのですか？

What have you _____ _____?

4. （驚いて）あなたはもう山田さんに会ったのですか？

Have you _____ _____ Mr. Yamada?

5. あなたは函館に行ったことがありますか？

Have you _____ been _____ Hakodate?

D Basic Composition

日本語を英語にしましょう。音声を聴いて正解を確認しましょう。))) Audio 61

1. 彼女は少し不安そうに見えます。何かあったのですか？

She _____ _____ _____ _____. Is there _____ _____ with her?

2. 奨学金のおかげで私は大学を卒業できた。

_____ _____ _____ _____, I could graduate from college.

3. 私たちの提案はついにその委員会によって受け入れられた。

Our proposal _____ _____ _____ _____ _____ at last.

4. 仕事が終わったら、集まりましょう。

_____ _____ _____ _____ we finish work.

5. 昨日はお手伝いをしていただき、どうもありがとうございました。

It _____ _____ _____ of _____ _____ _____ _____ yesterday.

E Composition

（　　）内の語を並べかえて日本語に合う英語にしましょう。大文字で始まる語句も小文字になっています。

1. ラフカディオ・ハーンは、1890 年に日本にやってきた放浪の詩人であった。

_____ came to Japan in 1890.

(poet / a / Lafcadio Hearn / who / wandering / was)

2. 彼らは遅れないように早く出発した。

They _____.
(order / be / not / left / of / to / late / early / in)

3. 物価はまた上がると言われている。

_____ again.

(said / are / rise / it / that / is / prices / going to)

4. ひとつミスをしたからといってけなすな。

Don't do me down _____.
(I / mistake / because / simply / one / made)

5. 結局、ほとんどの大学は研究を重要視しなくなった。

After all, _____.
(to / universities / have / few / emphasize / research / come)